Original title:
Lost in the Larch

Copyright © 2025 Creative Arts Management OÜ
All rights reserved.

Author: Jasper Montgomery
ISBN HARDBACK: 978-1-80567-215-9
ISBN PAPERBACK: 978-1-80567-514-3

Where Time Stands Still

The clock forgot to tick today,
As squirrels start their ballet play.
With acorns flying through the air,
I duck and weave, but do not care.

The sun is bright, the shadows wide,
Chasing my hat as if it tried.
Frogs croak gossip by the stream,
While I just laugh and start to dream.

Caress of the Morning Dew

Morning's kiss upon my nose,
Tickles from the grass that grows.
I dance with bees who buzz and sway,
While butterflies join in the fray.

A gentle breeze begins to tease,
As nature hums its quirky keys.
I stumble on a root, oh dear!
And now I'm rolling, full of cheer.

Beneath the Verdant Canopy

Trees are chatting, leaves in gossip,
I'm eavesdropping, it's a trip.
With branches stretching, waving wide,
I'm just a fool caught in the tide.

A woodpecker taps a silly beat,
I clap along with flapping feet.
As shadows dance in playful glee,
I make a fool of little me.

Harmonics of the Woods

The forest sings a quirky tune,
In harmony with clouds and moon.
With every chirp and rustle here,
I chuckle at the silly cheer.

A raccoon joins the jolly song,
Confident it won't go wrong.
As mushrooms stifle giggles low,
I trip and laugh, what a show!

Timeless Echoes of the Woodlands

A squirrel danced with my sandwich, oh dear,
It chattered and laughed like it knew I was near.
I chased with a grin, but my lunch was too fast,
He vanished with joy, I just stood there aghast.

The trees all snickered as I made a scene,
With the ants in a conga, so proud and so keen.
They waved tiny flags, oh what a parade,
While I tried to find where my dignity strayed.

A woodpecker teased with a rhythmic tap-tap,
My head did a dance, what a curious clap.
With the birds as my chorus, they filled up the air,
While I spun in circles, a sight they could share.

In shadows of laughter, the mushrooms all grew,
They whispered sweet secrets on what I should do.
With each little giggle, I tripped on a root,
And the trees laughed in chorus, "Oh, look at the brute!"

So if you should wander where giggles are loud,
And the squirrels are kings, strutting proud in the crowd,
Just remember to laugh, take a trip through the green,
For the joy is eternal, in every scene.

An Invitation from the Pines

The pines are giving hugs too tight,
Their branches tickle with delight.
Come dance with squirrels, join the fun,
We'll have a party 'til we see the sun.

The pine cones drop like silly bombs,
They land on heads, creating qualms.
The forest laughs at our surprise,
As we all giggle 'neath the skies.

Mice hold a feast on velvet beds,
While chatting softly 'bout their breads.
Join us, dance in circles, twirl,
In this piney paradise, give it a whirl.

In the Arms of the Forest

The trees are like a cozy crowd,
Each whispering secret, singing loud.
With roots that trip and branches that sway,
Come join their antics, what do you say?

A raccoon sings a high-pitched tune,
While beetles jive 'neath the light of the moon.
The mushrooms giggle in shades of bright,
Painting the forest with pure delight.

The leaves are clapping, can you hear?
They cheer for every squirrel and deer.
Together we frolic, chase shadows and glare,
In the arms of the woods, without a care.

Mysteries of the Green World

The ferns are hiding tic-tac-toe,
While snails are slow, but they steal the show.
The gnarly roots twist into knots,
Where creatures plot their silly thoughts.

There's a map drawn with a dandelion's fluff,
Leading us all to a treasure of stuff.
But who needs gold when laughter's the prize?
The fawns are backflipping, oh what a surprise!

Worms throw parties under the ground,
Quite the ruckus, but no one's around.
Join the fest, leap, and sway,
In this green world, we'll laugh all day.

A Journey away from the Ordinary

Pack your bags with giggles and cheer,
Leave behind worries and any fear.
The trail is sparkly, the path is bright,
Adventures await, oh what a sight!

The rabbits are racing on tiny tracks,
While hedgehogs plan a dance party to relax.
We'll swing with vines and climb trees tall,
In this whimsical world, come one, come all!

We'll paint the sky with shades of fun,
Chasing the rays of the glowing sun.
Life's just a ride in this playful land,
Join us now, take my hand!

A Whispering Reverie

In the woods where the trees sing,
Squirrels in jackets dance and swing.
Nature's wonders, quirky and bright,
Trees gossip secrets, day and night.

A raccoon wears a crown of twigs,
While rabbits hop with tiny gigs.
Branches sway, as if in jest,
Telling tales at their leafy fest.

Each shadow's thrown in funny shapes,
Playful tricks by nature's drapes.
The paths weave stories, twist and twirl,
Underneath, the wild critters whirl.

With laughter echoing through the air,
Even the toads have flair to spare.
Nature's jesters in a leafy crowd,
Join the fun, be merry and loud!

Palette of Leaves

A splash of color paints the ground,
In shades of laughter, joy abound.
Leaves tumble down with a giggly cheer,
Each one whispers, 'Come play here!'

Green, orange, and sunny gold,
Stories of autumn yet untold.
Froggy hats and acorn cups,
Bring your friends, let's drink it up!

The wind plays tricks, nudges us near,
Swirling dancers chime, 'Over here!'
Laughter tickles the breezy maze,
What a day, through this leafy haze!

Every rustle hides a joke or pun,
Swaying branches bask in the sun.
Life's a canvas where we take part,
In this merry gallery of heart!

Treading in Stillness

A crunch beneath my wobbly feet,
I greet a squirrel, what a treat!
In quiet corners, mischief breeds,
As critters plot their nutty deeds.

The mossy ground is soft and sly,
Hiding secrets that flutter by.
A turtle drags its shell in glee,
'Slowest racer, come catch me!'

The stillness carries whims and quirks,
Where every shadow silently lurks.
Mushrooms giggle, hiding their heads,
Whispering jokes while dodging threads.

Each footfall adds to nature's rhyme,
Time stands still, oh what a climb!
Underneath the leafy veil,
Adventure's found on this grand trail!

The Solace of Leafy Shadows

In leafy patches, shadows play,
Tickling toes that dare to stray.
With every rustle, laughter looms,
As critters pop from hidden rooms.

The sun peeks through with a cheeky grin,
Joking with me, "Where have you been?"
I giggle back, while squirrels tease,
Hiding acorns with utmost ease.

A game of tag with a wrinkled snail,
Replacing speed with a funny tale.
Air is filled with delightful dance,
As bugs toss about in a merry trance.

Underneath this canopy of cheer,
Nature's stories we hold dear.
In shadows deep, we find the light,
Filled with giggles, our hearts take flight!

Voices of the Whispering Firs

The trees were chattering, oh what a sight,
I swear one called me, 'Hey, what's your plight?'
A squirrel chimed in, with a flick of a tail,
'You think you're special? I've got a big sale!'

Their gossip was juicy, like berries in bloom,
'These hikers are wacky, they dance like a broom!'
I laughed so hard, I tripped on a root,
'Guess it's time to learn how to switch my cute boots!'

A Dance with the Dappled Sun

The sun peeked through, like a cheeky sprite,
'Try dancing with shadows, it feels just right!'
I wiggled my toes, feeling quite spry,
But tripped on my shoelace, oh me, oh my!

The beams were laughing, I could swear they grinned,
Spinning round and round, till I thought I'd sinned.
Then a bird joined in, what a fancy prance,
Together we jigged—what a fumble of chance!

Where Dreams Meet Roots

Beneath the boughs, I took a long nap,
Awoke with a start, thought I'd missed the map.
Dreams whispered loudly, 'The snack time is near!'
I searched for a sandwich, but found a deer!

It blinked with confusion, then gave me a grin,
'You look rather lost—want to try a spin?'
We twirled 'round the trunks, a clumsy parade,
'Thoroughly delightful,' I blurted, amazed!

Journey to the Heart of Solitude

I ventured alone, seeking silence and peace,
Instead found some critters, their chatter won't cease.
They all had a party, threw acorns in cheer,
'We're glad you could join us, please don't disappear!'

With nuts flying 'round like confetti from space,
I laughed at their antics, what a raucous place!
In solitude's grip, I was utterly found,
Amongst all the laughter, it was joy all around!

A Journey to the Heart of Green

In the woods where squirrels play,
I got tangled in some hay.
The trees all giggled, what a scene,
As I tripped over something green.

A bird laughed, perched up so high,
I asked it, "What's the reason why?"
It chirped back with a cheeky grin,
"Just watch your step, you're stepping in!"

The branches danced in the breeze,
While I was clinging to my knees.
I waved to friends, they waved back, too,
But my foot found a muddy shoe!

So here I stand, a sight so grand,
With mossy socks, it was not planned.
Yet through the laughter and the fun,
I found joy, now I'm on the run!

Echoes of the Tall Ones

Tall ones whisper secrets near,
As I drink my forest beer.
They say, "Oh dear, don't make a sound,"
But I tripped and hit the ground!

Every echo laughs at me,
Shouting, "You're too clumsy, see?"
Yet the leaves dance, wild and free,
Inviting me to join the spree.

I tried to climb one with great flair,
But ended up just hanging there.
"Don't worry," spoke a friendly pine,
"Just grab my branch, you'll be just fine!"

So I swung like a forest king,
With branches bending, made me swing.
Though my fashion sense needs some work,
In this greenscape, I'm not a jerk!

Beneath the Canopy of Time

Beneath the boughs, I lost my grin,
Staring up at roots within.
The trees giggled, sharing tales,
As I slid down on leafy trails.

Sap dripped down like sweetened talk,
I thought I'd take a silly walk.
A toad leaped up, gave me a jest,
I laughed so hard, fell on a nest!

"Hey there, buddy, it's a odd view,
With mud on your face, who are you?"
I puffed out my chest, said, "I'm a scout,
Exploring the woods, with no doubt!"

So gather 'round, we'll sing a song,
Where the plants dance, and nothing's wrong.
In this maze of green and rhyme,
My heartbeats echo, lost in time!

The Path Less Traveled

I took a path that swerved and spun,
Thought it would bring me lots of fun.
But vines wrapped tight like a twisty game,
Hollering out, "What's your name?"

A squirrel scolded, "You're all askew,
Why not follow the trail that's true?"
But I was stuck in leafy chains,
While nature laughed at my silly pains.

I waved to bushes, they waved back,
In the thicket, I lost my track.
A rabbit winked, it knew the way,
But I preferred my hop-and-sway!

With every misstep, joy unfurled,
As the laughter echoed through my world.
So here I roam with whimsy bright,
In the wild where wrong feels right!

Enigma of the Forest's Heart

In the woods, a squirrel pranced,
Chasing shadows, it danced and danced.
A wandering gnome, with a tiny hat,
Asked the trees where he could chat.

Out jumped a rabbit with a squeaky cheer,
"What is a gnome?" it asked in fear.
The trees whispered tales of yore,
Of a secret hideout behind the door.

The gnome scratched his head, lost in thought,
"I was just looking for a party, I thought!"
The rabbit rolled its eyes, oh so bright,
"Good luck finding friends in this dim light!"

Undeterred, the little gnome sighed,
With every step, he'd take it in stride.
For amidst the whispers and rustling sound,
There are mysteries here, waiting to be found.

Hallowed Ground under Pine

Beneath the pines, a picnic laid,
With sandwiches stacked, a grand charade.
A raccoon peered with some envy and glee,
"Where's my share of your lunch, oh me?"

The humans laughed, they shared a bite,
As the raccoon's eyes gleamed, oh what a sight.
"I'll join your crew, just for fun!"
Said the sneaky friend who weighed a ton.

A throwaway cap flew up in the air,
Caught in branches, no one could dare.
The raccoon chortled, waving his paw,
"That's a fine hat! You'll look like a straw!"

Amidst the laughter, the sun dipped low,
In the hallowed woods, where good times grow.
For under the pines, they shared a spark,
Creating memories that lit the dark.

A Place Between the Trees

In a glade, a sign read, 'Welcome, my friend!'
Beneath the branches, let laughter blend.
A fox donned glasses, pondering a tome,
"Who wrote this? I thought I'd stay home!"

The deer took a sip from the babbling brook,
"Is this a school? Give me a book!"
But the rabbit giggled with snacks in its pouch,
"It's just a party, come on, let's slouch!"

They gathered around for a tale or two,
With owls giving wisdom, a scholarly crew.
The fox then asked, "What's the moral of this?"
"It's simple," the deer said, "Just don't miss bliss!"

So they danced and pranced, in giggles and cheer,
In a place where the trees turned laughter to beer.
Forget the rules, let whimsy shine through,
For joy lies in moments, shared between two.

The Call of the Wildwood

The wind howled loudly, a mischievous tease,
As squirrels debated who'd climb the tallest trees.
A bear in a jacket, so snug and absurd,
Shouted, "Let's party! Who's in for a bird?"

The birds tweeted back, "We're busy right now,
Feeding our hatchlings, oh my, what a row!"
But the bear wasn't worried, he just brought a cake,
"Who can say no to this sweet, tasty flake?"

Then came a raccoon with a tap on the drum,
"Let's make some noise, or we just might succumb!"
The trees swayed gently to the rhythm and beat,
As night fell upon them, a comic retreat.

So under the stars, they sang silly tunes,
While the moon watched with joy, peeking through runes.
In the wildwood's heart, where laughter was found,
Life was a riddle, blissfully unbound.

The Forgotten Pathway

In a forest where squirrels conspire,
I tripped on a root, sparked by desire.
The path twisted laughably, oh what a sight,
With each step I took, my shoes felt too tight.

I wandered 'round trees with faces so wise,
They whispered of secrets, they'd giggle, and sigh.
I asked for directions, they rolled their eyes wide,
And offered me acorns, not help, as my guide.

Voices of the Ancient Trees

The trees held a meeting, I crept away shy,
They chatted in circles, beneath clouds so high.
One claimed to hold wisdom of ages gone past,
While another just hummed, making a laugh that was vast.

I leaned in to hear, what they planned for the day,
But all they discussed was a bird's ballet.
With branches a-waving, they danced quite absurd,
I joined in their frolic, all worries deterred.

In Search of Wooded Dreams

I ventured for dreams wrapped in green wraps,
But found only squirrels and their loud little chats.
They giggled at me as I searched for the way,
To chase down the whimsy that led me astray.

I asked a sly fox for a map to my quest,
He offered me cheese and a nap—what a jest!
I chuckled and thanked him, then tumbled away,
In a woodland of laughter, I'd happily stay.

Fragments of a Green Memory

In a glade that was sounding with laughter and cheer,
I talked to a mushroom who claimed he'd been here.
He giggled and shimmied, with spores all a-twirl,
Said he knew all the gossip within this green world.

We danced in the sunlight on soft, leaf-filled mats,
Discussed all the legends of long-forgotten bats.
With each silly story, I felt peace descend,
For in this green haven, I found a true friend.

Reflections in the Shade

Sunbeams dance on bark and leaf,
Chasing shadows, a comic relief.
Squirrels chatter, plotting their schemes,
As I trip on roots, lost in dreams.

With every step, a giggle bursts,
A deer looks on, eyes about to burst.
My coffee spills, oh what a sight,
Guess today, the forest's got bite!

A wobbly owl swoops just too low,
It hoots at me, 'Hey, take it slow!'
I nod like a fool, brush off the dirt,
Just a typical day, I'm used to the hurt.

Bee in the breeze, buzzing with flair,
It's a waltz gone wild, in the open air.
Nature chuckles, while I make a dive,
Who knew the trees had such a lively vibe?

Through the Thicket's Embrace

In the thicket, a tangle of dreams,
Branches wave like they're in teams.
A rabbit hops by, all spry and neat,
While I trip over twigs, oh what a feat!

Between the ferns, a creeping vine,
Whispers to me, 'Your sense of time?'
With laughter that echoes, it pulls at my sleeve,
'You'll find your way if you just believe!'

A chorus of birds joins the jest,
One squawks 'Surprise!' and I take a rest.
I catch a glimpse of a deer with flair,
Sipping water, only to stare!

Through the shadows, I dance and glide,
With trees as my partners, in a funny ride.
So here's to the path, wherever it leads,
In this thicket of laughter, where humor feeds.

The Stillness that Speaks

The forest pauses, but humor's alive,
Crickets chirp, like they're ready to jive.
A statue of moss on an old log grins,
Guess it's seen all my silly sins.

Barking beetles have their own gossip,
While in my backpack, snacks do slip.
A family of ants throws a tiny parade,
Marching right past — they've certainly stayed!

And what of the wind? It tickles the trees,
Trying hard to make me sneeze.
In the stillness, a chuckle escapes,
Nature's own punchline, in silly shapes.

So here in this hush, life never grows old,
With whispers of laughter that twist and unfold.
In silent moments, a riddle survives,
Where giggles of nature truly thrive.

Twilight's Tapestry

Dusk weaves a thread, golden and sassy,
Creatures emerge, both shy and classy.
A fox sneezes loud, and I can't resist,
How did it know I just made a list?

Fireflies flicker, like tiny lamps,
Summoning mischief in their little camps.
I attempt a stroll, but who should I see?
A raccoon winks, 'Join the jamboree!'

Crickets compose a clumsy song,
While I hum along — it can't be wrong.
A turtle just laughs, slow as can be,
Saying, 'Life's a race, but what's the fee?'

As twilight settles, and shadows bend,
I find humor in trails that twist and blend.
Under this canvas, a laugh and a sigh,
In twilight's tapestry, we'll flutter and fly.

Breath of the Ancient Trees

In the woods where whispers play,
Trees laugh and sway all day.
Squirrels gossip, quite absurd,
While I ponder every word.

Roots tickle toes that wander wide,
The ancient bark seems full of pride.
Branches wave like a friendly greeting,
Nature's humor, never fleeting.

Mossy hats upon the ground,
Each step takes me round and round.
A dance of shadows, light, and mist,
In this place I can't resist.

Every leaf a trickster's grin,
With secrets deep—where to begin?
Echoes of laughter all around,
In this grove, joy can be found.

Solitude in the Woods

Amidst the trees so tall and stout,
I feel surrounded yet, no doubt.
Bark chuckles as I trip and slip,
Nature's joke, I can't outstrip.

The silence teases, starts to hum,
While squirrels mock—oh, here they come!
Pine needles whisper in a rush,
Like nature's own little hush-hush.

Branches bend to eavesdrop low,
As I attempt a clumsy show.
Dancing with shadows, wild and free,
I laugh along with this old tree.

In solitude, I'm not alone,
With laughter carved in nature's bone.
Every rustle a friendly call,
In this space, I feel quite small.

Between Boughs and Silence

Between the boughs, I hear the tease,
Of rustling leaves swaying in the breeze.
Chirping birds throw jokes on high,
While acorns drop with a playful sigh.

A wandering deer gives me a look,
As if I've wandered from a book.
It shakes its head, a knowing wink,
As if to say, "We need to think."

Mushrooms giggle, sprouting bold,
In colors bright, a sight to behold.
Each step forward, I grin and spin,
Among the trees, I find my kin.

The humor here is soft and sly,
With nature's pranks that never die.
In this quiet, I laugh aloud,
Among the trees, I'm heartily proud.

The Hidden Trail

On the path less traveled, I stumble and trip,
Following roots like a playful script.
A path of laughter, twist and twine,
Where each turn leads to an old pine.

Beneath the branches, secrets swirl,
As breezes tickle, leaves unfurl.
A path so wild, yet I feel bold,
Every step, a story told.

I spot a fox in a hat of grass,
With a cheeky grin as he lets me pass.
"Where are you going?" he seems to jest,
"In circles, I see, like all the rest."

With every corner, a chuckle grows,
As nature's wit in fun shows.
In the hidden trail, I laugh and roam,
In the heart of trees, I've found my home.

Muffled Steps in the Undergrowth

Beneath the trees, my foot slipped,
I squealed like a pig, oh what a trip!
A squirrel chuckled, perched up high,
While branches waved like they'd say goodbye.

The moss wore my shoes like a scarf,
As I stumbled and tumbled, it made me laugh.
A raccoon's grin, like a mask in the night,
Watched my ballet of clumsiness take flight.

A dance with the ferns, oh how they twirl,
With arms full of leaves, I gave them a whirl.
The pine cones giggled, green sap did flow,
In this forest of folly, I stole the show.

Silhouettes of Evening

Shadows creep as daylight wanes,
My silhouette trips over nature's chains.
The owls hoot while I try to prance,
With a head full of dreams and white-knuckled pants.

I thought I saw a ghostly hare,
Turns out it was just my wild hair!
Branches tangled, my arms ablaze,
In a forest so thick, a sticky maze.

I waved at the stars in a friendly way,
But bats mistook me for a buffet!
Laughter echoes through the pitch-black night,
As I dodge tree roots with all my might.

Through the Dimmed Light

In dimmed light where owls play peek,
I ventured forth to hear them speak.
But tangled roots, they plotted a jest,
I tripped and tumbled, who knew they'd jest?

A lantern bug blinked, oh what a laugh,
Switched on my path like a silly photograph.
"I'm not a moth!" I yelled in vain,
While twigs lost their battle, I felt some pain.

Dancing with shadows, I made a scene,
Pretending I'm cool, though I'm far from keen.
The gnarled old trees just shook their heads,
While mushrooms laughed, "Off with her threads!"

Wishes Carved in Wood

With a knife and dreams, I carved my plea,
On a soft oak plank, beneath a large tree.
"Make me graceful," I whispered real low,
But the wood just grinned and said, "Oh, no!"

Each groove held secrets of who I wished to be,
Yet the squirrels stole wishes, quite sneakily.
They held a council, tails all a-fluff,
And laughed at my hopes, saying, "That's tough!"

The knots in the grain, they knotted my fate,
Where laughter grew wild, I'd dance and bait.
With each silly wish, I felt so alive,
In this forest of folly, I'll always survive.

The Enigma of the Wandering Footsteps

A footstep here, a footstep there,
Where'd they go? I just can't bear.
Leaves are laughing, a rustle, a tease,
Socks don't match, oh mom, where's my keys?

A squirrel points left, then gestures right,
Am I the punchline? This feels not right.
Chasing shadows, I trip on my lace,
I'm just a jester in this silly chase.

Follow the giggles, that's what I'll do,
But every step feels like déjà vu.
The ground's a joker, it's acting so sly,
Is this a forest or a circus I spy?

In the woods where the trees love to sham,
With branches waving like a mangy ham.
I'll find my way back, or so I say,
With a map drawn in jellybeans, on my way!

Beneath the Boughs of Silence

Beneath the trees, there's a raucous hush,
Is that a twig snap? Or just a bush?
Whispers of the fauna, a secretive crew,
Informing the wind, I haven't a clue.

A fox reads the news, on a log, quite absurd,
While owls play charades, it's all so blurred.
Caterpillars gossip in philosophical tones,
Debating the merits of twigs versus stones.

Suddenly sneezing, I startle a deer,
With more grace than me, it just disappears.
A chuckle erupts from the nearby tree,
I swear they're laughing at my clumsiness spree.

In this field of silence, I search for my rhymes,
But the only sound is the chimes of the chimes.
Stumbling through laughter, I'll leave my mark,
A dance with the shadows, a humorous lark.

The Hymn of the Aged Timber

The old trees groan like a talkative chap,
Telling tales as I take a nap.
Their bark has wrinkles, full of old jokes,
Yet here I stand, as they bicker and poke.

Lichen is laughing, it's hard to believe,
This timber is wiser; I'm just here to grieve.
A squirrel does ballet on a branch above,
While I'm clumsily tripping, where's the love?

The shade shimmies, seeking attention anew,
But I'm the main act, wearing mismatched shoes.
Greener grasses chuckle, as I take a bow,
A performance of folly, do I take a vow?

With roots so deep, yet limbs swaying free,
The trees cheer for me, a glorious spree.
One more step, let's hope I don't break,
It's the chorus of laughter that I now take.

Under the Shade of Solitude

Under the canopy, where shadows conspire,
I sit with the crickets, sipping on ire.
Sunlight like giggles, spills through the leaves,
While ants in a line play puppet thieves.

Around every corner, a laugh lurks near,
The sun's a prankster, the trees a seer.
I try to be quiet, but my stomach sings,
A rumble, a tumble, comedy it brings.

A butterfly flutters with graceful delight,
Teasing my instincts to join in the flight.
But here I will stay, a statue of bliss,
Caught in the riddle of the forest's kiss.

With shadows for company, I ponder awhile,
The mysteries of nature woven with style.
One foot behind, I try to be bold,
But stumbling through laughter, is the tale to be told.

Songs of the Lonesome Cedar

In a grove where the tall trees sway,
A squirrel sings both night and day.
His voice is funny, a croaky tone,
He claims he's king, all alone.

The raccoons dance, a silly jig,
While birch trees chuckle, so big, so big.
A fox rolls by, in comedic flair,
Trips on twigs, but doesn't care.

Underneath a sky of playful hues,
The owls hoot clever, sharing news.
They gossip tales of falling leaves,
As laughter echoes through the eaves.

So here amid the woods we find,
Nature's antics, sweet and blind.
A giggle here, a snort over there,
In the trees, there's love and care.

Into the Thicket's Embrace

Through tangled paths where brambles twist,
An owl flaps by, impossibly missed.
A porcupine rolls, what a sight!
He's face-first down, but that's alright.

Beneath the boughs, the shadows play,
A rabbit hops and then runs away.
With floppy ears and a twitching nose,
He laughs it off, in playful prose.

The bushes burst with chirps and sounds,
An orchestra of nature surrounds.
The hedgehogs giggle as they doth pose,
Pretending to be rocks, who knows?

In this embrace of greens and browns,
The woodland critters wear their crowns.
Amidst the fun, let's all rejoice,
For in the thicket, we find our voice.

The Unseen Trail

At dawn, explorers head out bold,
Yet every step, a tale unfolds.
A raccoon with snacks slips on a stone,
His cackle echoes, he's not alone.

The path grows wild with twists and bends,
Each turn bringing peculiar friends.
A chipmunk performs, a stand-up act,
Jokes on the trees, that's a fact!

The sunlight dances through the leaves,
As laughter floats, the heart believes.
A bear hums softly, out of key,
A melody lost in comic glee.

So onward we march, with cheer and flair,
Through unseen trails, with friends we share.
The woods may fool us, but we find,
All's well when love's aligned.

Beneath a Canopy of Uncertainty

Underneath leaves that decide to drop,
A squirrel plots mischief, never to stop.
He hides his acorns, a sneaky game,
But he forgets where he put the same.

The wind whips up, and all seems lost,
A wily fox considers the cost.
He chases shadows, now what a fuss,
His plans may bust, but he's never thus!

Amidst the fun of nature's play,
A bear rolls in with a loud hooray.
His belly's round, he claims the prize,
Of pie in the sky, oh how he tries!

Beneath this canopy, unsure yet bright,
The laughter lingers, pure delight.
For in this dance of silly chance,
We spin and twirl in nature's dance.

Secrets in the Evergreen

In a forest of needles, my map's gone astray,
The squirrels are giggling, as I bumble and sway.
Trees whisper secrets, oh what could they mean?
I swear one just winked—this must be a dream!

Moss-covered rocks peek at my misfit parade,
I trip on a root, oh what a fine spade!
Fungi are snickering, I'm sure it's a jest,
While branches above play a game of who's best.

With humor and chaos, this path is a tease,
I stumble on laughter, I tumble with ease.
The shadows are dancing, they keep me in check,
Just when I think I'm on the right track, I'm a wreck!

Yet every wrong turn feels oddly like fun,
The trees chirp their giggles, they can't be outdone.
So here's to the journey, wherever it leads,
In this patch of green chaos, I'll gather my seeds.

A Journey Through Misty Groves

Wandering through fog, my compass is shot,
Is that a gnome waving, or'm I seeing a lot?
These trees are so tall, they could reach for the sky,
I'm just here to frolic, it's not the time to cry!

The path turns to mush, like pudding on ground,
I laugh at my boots, oh, how they have drowned!
Each step is a splash, like a giant's big prank,
And the critters all smirk from their leafy old bank.

Amidst the thick mist, I make friends with a crow,
He quips 'Everything's fine, just follow the flow!'
I give him a nod, though I know he won't guide,
He seems just as lost—ah, it's fun to abide!

So here in the grove, let's giggle and whirl,
The mysteries beckon, it's a whimsical swirl.
With jest and bright smiles, we'll navigate right,
Tomorrow we'll laugh at the maze of the night.

Sylvan Reveries

In shadows of trees, I trip on my dreams,
The whispers of branches are wacky, it seems!
Pinecones like soldiers stand guard on the floor,
While bushes hum tunes of a nutty folklore.

A squirrel's my guide, and he darts to and fro,
He's plotting a treasure, or maybe just show?
With acorns as tokens, we barter and trade,
Each giggle a prize in this forest charade.

The light filters down, like a shimmer of gold,
Yet all I can think of is laughter and bold.
I dance with the shadows, I leap like a sprite,
In this camp of the jolly, all wrongs turn to right.

So here's to the folly in sylvan delight,
With squirrels as my comrades, the day's out of sight.
I wave to the sun, as I bid it adieu,
For secrets in woodlands are better with two!

Beneath the Emerald Veil

Beneath tangled branches, I wander with glee,
The trees are like giants, no help I can see!
I slide on a trail that resembles a slip,
And twirl like a top on this whimsical trip.

A chorus of chortles springs up from the pines,
As insects compose an offbeat of lines.
The sun gleams like a spotlight on me,
I'm the star of an act that no one can see.

I bounce off the bark and get caught in a thorn,
The trees share a laugh, hey, they're never forlorn!
While mischief runs wild in this emerald scene,
I play hide and seek with the squirrels and leaves.

So here's to the laughter that fills up each seam,
A wild, winding forest, a never-ending dream.
With joy and confusion, we dance in a whirl,
In this tapestry of green, life's a giggling pearl!

Conversations with the Wind

I asked the breeze where it had been,
It laughed and said, 'You've seen my kin.'
Trees wave their arms, a playful show,
As I tripped on roots that wouldn't let go.

The gusts tell tales of squirrels that play,
Stealing acorns, they dash away.
I chase their shadows, but who would win?
The trees just giggle with leaves in spin.

A whisper floats, 'Join the game!' they tease,
I trip on twigs as I try to seize.
The wind, it mocks, with a gentle huff,
'Keep up, dear friend, it's just funny stuff!'

Yet in this chaos, I find a grace,
Nature's jest makes a cheerful space.
In this playful waltz, I'm lost and found,
Chasing the joy that dances around.

The Solace of Hidden Clearings

In a secret nook where laughter grows,
I found a spot that nobody knows.
The critters throw parties, wild and loud,
With acorns as snacks, they feast and crowd.

I asked a rabbit for the party plan,
He winked and said, 'Just be a fan.'
As I prepared, I bungled the snacks,
The ducks all quacked, 'Look who's lost tracks!'

The clearing's a circus, a sight to see,
With dancing leaves and a bumblebee.
They laugh as I tumble over a root,
In this wild gaiety, I find my loot.

With giggles and snorts, we share a toast,
To all the goofs that matter the most.
In this frolic, amidst the ferns,
I learn that laughter is what returns.

Through the Veils of Time

I wandered through ages where shadows blend,
Twisted and tangles, where trees pretend.
The time-twisted paths sport quirky signs,
Pointing me to places where humor shines.

I met a ghost with a penchant for pranks,
He played with the echoes; he pulled my flanks!
'What's time?' I asked the oak with charm,
It chuckled low and said, 'Come to harm!'

I saw a fox wearing a top hat grand,
Claiming the forest was his own land.
With a wink, he disappeared in a flash,
Leaving me laughing, a silly mishmash.

Through laughter and folly, time slips away,
In this merry chase, I've found my stay.
With whispers of giggles the trees align,
In this breezy journey, I bumble, but shine.

Whispers at Twilight's Edge

At twilight's gate where shadows prance,
I heard the trees in a goofy dance.
The stars peek out with a wink and blink,
As the crickets chirp, and the fireflies think.

The night unfolds like a storybook,
With every whisper, a curious look.
I asked the owl, 'What's the scoop tonight?'
He hooted back, 'Just take flight!'

A raccoon juggled some shiny things,
While the moon softly laughed, and the night still sings.
I stumbled and rolled on the cool, soft moss,
And the tree roots snickered, 'What a gloss!'

In this comical realm at the day's end,
I feel like a joke in the night's blend.
With giggles aflame and whispers in air,
At twilight's edge, I dance without a care.

Whispers Among the Pines

I heard a tree laugh, oh what a sound,
It tickled my ears as I fell to the ground.
Squirrels held court, in their nutty attire,
Debating the best ways to climb ever higher.

The branches all danced in a whimsical way,
Telling me jokes that brightened my day.
With each little gust, they'd sway to and fro,
As if they conspired to put on a show.

A pinecone flew past, like a rocket on track,
While one over there shouted, "Hey, watch your back!"
I chuckled and grinned, enjoying the spree,
Among all the giggles, I thought, "Aha! Me!"

So here in the woods, where the fun is afoot,
I'll dance with the trees in my very best suit.
For laughter and joy are my true guiding stars,
In a forest of fun, I'll forget my old cars.

Echoes of a Wandering Heart

My heart took a trip, with no map or guide,
It wandered through branches, all full of pride.
Bumped into a rabbit, so fluffy and spry,
Who offered advice, then hopped on by.

I followed a squirrel, so clever and spry,
He spilled all his secrets, then flitted to fly.
The trees played a tune, all rustles and shifts,
My heart danced along, to the rhythm of gifts.

With echoes of laughter and rustling leaves,
Each step on the path brought new tricks up their sleeves.
A pine tree spoke softly, "Don't hurry, dear friend,
There's magic in wandering, a joy without end."

So I twirled in delight, as I found my own thread,
With laughter and whispers, I was joyfully led.
Through woods wide and funny, my heart ran so free,
In the whispers and echoes, I found mystery.

Shadows Beneath the Canopy

Beneath leafy shadows, where silence is loud,
I tiptoed with caution, feeling quite proud.
But something went crack, oh what could that be?
A raccoon rolled by, just laughing at me!

The trees formed a maze, all twisted and bent,
They giggled at me, oh what a lament!
When I took a wrong turn, they whispered, "Hey you!
That's the way to the picnic, not the dust of the dew."

A shadow jumped out, it was just a big frog,
And he croaked out a riddle, 'cause he's quite the blog.
"Why did the leaf fall? To see what's below!"
I laughed in approval, as the answers would flow.

So deep in the shades, with the shadows I played,
In a world so absurd, under branches I stayed.
With humor surrounding, and giggles to part,
I found endless joy, deep within my own heart.

Regret of the Wayward Soul

I wandered too far, on this muddled old trail,
Chasing down butterflies, regaled with a tale.
The flowers all chimed in, "Come join in our dance!"
While I tripped and tumbled, with true lack of grace.

A wise old turtle said, "Slow down there friend,
This forest is tricky, you don't want it to end."
But I waved him away, thought I knew best,
Then fell in a puddle — oh, what a jest!

The trees burst with laughter, their trunks shaking wide,
"Don't worry, young sprout, we're all on your side!"
Regret? Not quite; just a laugh in the mire,
With squirrels providing a comedic choir.

So if you feel lost, don't let it bring gloom,
Embrace every stumble, let laughter consume.
For within all the mishaps and journeys we hold,
Are stories worth telling, and memories bold.

Enchantment of the Unseen Woods

In forests deep where shadows play,
A squirrel's nut went rolling away.
I chased it down, through twist and bends,
But all I found were laughing friends.

They pointed high, up at a branch,
Beneath it lay my silly stance.
I'd missed the nuts, and what a roar,
As deer and rabbits laughed some more.

I danced around with branches thick,
A tree trunk gave my leg a kick.
Echoes of joy rang through the air,
As woodland critters showed their flair.

So if you wander, heed my song,
The woods may list the world as wrong.
Yet in the jest of nature's arts,
A cheerful spirit never parts.

The Wayward Traveler's Lament

A map in hand, I set my stride,
But all I found was a big old slide.
Down I tumbled, all in a heap,
So much for treasures I'd hoped to reap.

With rabbits laughing, I tried to stand,
As twigs and thorns played a tricksy hand.
A grand adventure, or so I thought,
Twisted paths left me quite distraught.

The pine trees formed a comedy club,
As I recited my silly blub.
They whispered jokes, I laughed till I cried,
With every gust, my worries denied.

A winding path, I took a chance,
But ended up in a squirrel's dance.
While I may wander, confused and dazed,
The joy of folly keeps me amazed.

Whispers among the Pines

Among the pines, I lost my way,
They giggled softly, come what may.
Branches bowed in a jolly croon,
As I stepped on a sticky prune.

The ground was slick, a slapstick game,
With every tumble, I found my fame.
The thickets rustled, oh what a sight,
Squirrels applauded my clumsy plight.

A path appeared, but it led to pies,
Pine-cone treats in frosty skies.
I sampled crumbs from every tree,
A connoisseur of wild pastry.

So heed the laughs from branches above,
In green embraces, you find the love.
With every crack and silly fall,
The forest chuckles, welcoming all.

Shadows of the Timber

In shadows thick, I sought to roam,
But every step felt far from home.
A log rolled over, tripped me sight,
I landed softly, oh what a fright!

The trees conspired, creaking low,
They whispered secrets, oh what a show.
With branches waving like a band,
I opted for a conga stand.

With shadows dancing all around,
I spun and pranced upon the ground.
The woodlands chuckled, stout and bold,
Their humor worth more than any gold.

So if you wander where the shade,
Sings silly songs and never fade,
Just waltz along, forget the doom,
For laughter blooms within the gloom.

Lanterns in the Thicket

Underneath the foliage so thick,
A squirrel planned a little trick.
He wrapped a branch with lights so bright,
And danced around to his delight.

The owls blinked with such surprise,
As fireflies fell from the skies.
He giggled as he watched them fall,
In a woodland party, standing tall.

The rabbits joined, their ears a-flop,
While hedgehogs rolled and couldn't stop.
Laughter echoed through the trees,
A gathering of woodland decrees.

But when morning broke, oh what a sight,
The light was gone, the fun took flight.
And in the thicket, all was bare,
Except the memories hung in the air.

The Path of Regrets

With a map drawn from a nutty dream,
I stumbled on a creek that gleamed.
Each wrong turn made me scratch my head,
As talking mushrooms laughed instead.

I met a turtle who had lost his way,
He boldly stated, 'It's okay!'
But with each step, we spun in place,
Seeking wisdom but finding grace.

The path was winding, full of twists,
Where foggy shadows played at lists.
We tripped over roots and rolled in moss,
'At least we laugh,' I said, 'at our loss!'

And though our journey was quite absurd,
We found some joy in every word.
Tomorrow's adventure, we'll sort out,
For today we laugh, without a doubt.

Among the Glistening Needles

A pine cone fell like a heavy chunk,
It hit my head with a tiny thunk.
Surrounded by needles, I stood up tall,
And proclaimed, 'I'm king of them all!'

A raccoon chuckled from a nearby tree,
'Your crown's just for show, you see!'
He danced in circles, full of glee,
While I just shook off the debris.

The pine trees swayed with boughs that creaked,
They seemed to gossip, oh how they squeaked!
Among the glistening needles a dance,
I twirled like a fool, lost in my prance.

But then a breeze came, it was rude and bold,
Sweeping my crown from my head, oh so cold!
The laughter echoed, and I did swear,
Next time I'd not play debonair.

Echoing Lament of the Forest

The winds began a woeful song,
As I stumbled, where things felt wrong.
With branches pointing every way,
I felt the forest laugh and sway.

A fox declared, 'You're late for tea!'
'What foolish eyes, to wander free!'
But all I found were giggles stout,
As whispers turned to shouts about.

The owls put on a puppet show,
With crickets chirping high and low.
I sat enchanted, forgetting my flight,
In a play of shadows, comedic delight.

But as the dusk began to fall,
I wondered if I'd seen it all.
The echoes of laughter swirled around,
In this jolly forest, lost but found.

A Solitary Song in the Woods

In the forest so dense and deep,
A squirrel sings, but I can't keep.
His high-pitched notes make bees retreat,
While I try to dance to this silly beat.

The trees all sway, like they're in a trance,
While I trip over roots, missing my chance.
I'm looking for wisdom from angry crows,
But they just laugh at my clumsy shows.

A raccoon joins in, with a cheeky grin,
Stealing my snacks, oh where to begin?
So I laugh and sigh, toss my hands in the air,
This goofy ensemble is quite the affair!

Alone yet not, in this funny place,
With woodland pals, I've found my grace.
A melody plays, off-key and bright,
In the laughter of trees, my heart takes flight.

Between Bark and Breeze

A pinecone dropped, right on my head,
The trees above chuckled, I fled.
In this breezy space, where giggles grow,
I can hear them whisper, 'It's part of the show!'

The wind swirls round, like a playful tease,
While branches bow low, like they wish to please.
A chipmunk darts by, with a nut supreme,
Does he know he's the star of my daydream?

Stumbling on trails, I scratch my chin,
These thickets and branches, a real-tail win.
All the creatures conspire, with mischief in air,
In this whimsical dance, I haven't a care.

The laughter of rustling leaves takes flight,
In this woodland romp, everything feels right.
So I'll hum along, with my newfound friends,
In this wacky world, the fun never ends.

The Essence of Dappled Light

Sunlight flickers through leaves like a wink,
While I trip over shadows, take time to think.
In this patch of humor, where sunbeams play,
I wink back at nature; it's just our way!

Each step I take, the ground lets out a creak,
It's a comedy show, nature's unique peak.
With every stumble, my laugh echoes loud,
The trees join the chorus, they're surely proud!

A butterfly flutters, kicks up some dust,
In this dappled arena, it's a must.
With smiles and giggles, we form a brigade,
In the play of the forest, we're all unafraid.

So I'll bask in the glow of this quirky delight,
While shadows dance cool in the faded light.
It's a comedy sketch in a woodland retreat,
Where the essence of joy makes my day complete.

Cut from the same Branch

Two birds on a branch, sharing a chat,
One's gossiping loudly, the other's a brat.
As I stand underneath, with my mouth agape,
I can't help but laugh at their birdy escape.

A sturdy oak looks down, shaking its leaves,
Mumbling wise jokes only the forest believes.
I ponder my thoughts, in this nutty delight,
What wisdom is found in a bark-covered sight?

The squirrels conspire with a dash of flair,
Planning a heist for a single peanut fair.
With acrobatic leaps, they both pull a stunt,
In this trunk-clad circus, I'm enjoying the front!

Brothers and sisters, we're all part of the same,
In this grove of giggles, we each have a name.
So let's cherish the laughter, so wild and free,
For the trees and the critters have all come for tea!

Echoes through the Needles

Whispers dance among the trees,
A squirrel asks, "What's with the breeze?"
Branches sway in a giggling fit,
While a raccoon ties his little knit.

Frogs leap high, like tiny jesters,
Rooting for the local testers.
A fox sneezes, and oh what fun,
Startling mice, they dash and run.

The chipmunks cheer, it's quite the show,
As pinecones fall, above them go.
Laughter echoes through the leaves,
Even the grumpy owl believes!

With each rustle, a joke's been told,
The forest's secrets, brave and bold.
Echoes linger in leafy halls,
Where nature's humor never stalls.

A Mist in the Grove

In the grove, the fog rolls thick,
Was that a ghost? No, just a trick!
A rabbit hops, and he goes 'Boo!'
Startling friends with a spooky view.

The mist hangs low, like cotton candy,
A porcupine, he looks quite dandy.
With spikes like hair, he strikes a pose,
Then slips and tumbles – oh, how it goes!

Frogs croak jokes, with comedic flair,
Tickling the toads, they wiggle in air.
Fog dances off, a ghostly tease,
While lizards chuckle among the trees.

A whisper here, a laugh or two,
In the grove, there's much to view.
Mirth and mischief wrapped in haze,
In nature's world, we spend our days.

Secrets Beneath the Canopy

Underneath the leafy dome,
A worm hums tunes that feel like home.
Beneath the surface, jokes abound,
With mushrooms giggling all around.

Roots tickle toes of passing bears,
While ants insist they're millionaires!
The wise old trees, they chuckle and sway,
As whispers of secrets float away.

A hedgehog's grin, quite round and bright,
Saying, "Nature's humor is just right!"
With every leaf that flutters down,
It seems the forest wears a crown.

So listen close to the breezy song,
With laughter echoed all day long.
In the whispers of leaves and boughs,
The forest speaks, and so it vows!

Tread Softly on the Slope

Tread lightly where the pine trees lean,
Where acorns roll, like a playful scene.
A squirrel giggles, a bird takes flight,
As shadows dance in morning light.

Upon the slope, footfalls are sneaky,
A hedgehog yawns, his day feels cheeky.
A stumble here, a slip or fall,
And nature's chorus giggles through it all.

The sun peeks through, a cheeky grin,
A bouncing rabbit hops right in.
All around, the wildlife plays,
In this merry, woodland maze.

So tread softly, join the fun,
In the forest, we're all one.
With laughter lurking in every nook,
The world's a story, just take a look!

Unraveled in the Embrace of Nature

A squirrel wore my hat, oh what a sight,
He claimed it was his, said he's quite the knight.
Around the trees I stumbled, oh what a race,
Chasing my own shadow, losing my place.

The birds started laughing, they thought it a show,
As I tripped on a root—where'd that thing go?
Nature spun me 'round in her breezy embrace,
I swear I heard giggles from the soft mossy base.

Leaves tickled my ankles, what a silly parade,
While I danced with the ferns, in sunshine I stayed.
A raccoon played the drums, with acorns galore,
In the woods' grand cabaret, I asked for encore!

Then came a wise owl, the referee judge,
In a laughter-filled contest, I dared not to budge.
Underneath branches where bright laughter soars,
I'll return for more fun, through nature's own doors.

The Forgotten Glade

In the glade I found a shoe, one without a mate,
Was it left by a runner or perhaps a great date?
A trumpet vine giggled, swaying side to side,
I waved to a hedge, it chuckled and sighed.

The grass hummed a tune, not a care in the world,
While daisies threw confetti, laughter unfurled.
A gopher wore glasses, inspecting the scene,
I asked if he'd seen my lost screen machine!

A butterfly twirled, with flair it would boast,
Said it knew all the secrets of the glade's friendly ghost.
But all I got back was a wink and a nudge,
As I heard tree branches say, "Don't be a grudge!"

So here in this spot, I found out it's true,
Nature holds parties, just waiting for you.
With roots all a-tangle and laughter that sways,
I'll come back to this glade for the rest of my days.

Foliage Dreams

In a dream made of leaves, I prepared to take flight,
Where the trees played the tunes and the sun was my light.

I danced with the dandelions, what a silly waltz,
They laughed as I tripped, but it's not their fault!

Thistles told stories of the days long ago,
While mosses whispered secrets in tones soft and low.
The wind started chuckling, it knew it could tease,
As I stumbled through thickets, on my wobbly knees!

A rabbit with spectacles critiqued my wrong moves,
He chuckled and danced; oh, how he improves!
"Just follow my lead! Don't you trip over stones!"
But with my clumsy twirls, I sank into the loans.

In this vibrant ballet, where fun takes the helm,
I'll forever be twirling in foliage's realm.
With laughter as my guide, and trees as my friends,
This dream won't be ending, it only transcends!

Where the Light Dances

Under canopies bright, where shadows play tag,
I spotted a mouse, with a tiny green flag.
"Join me!" he squeaked, in a whispering tone,
As the sunlight embraced us, we blurred through the grove.

There were giggles of squirrels in the shimmering air,
With nutty confessions, without any care.
As the dappled light fluttered, I started to spin,
In a delightful dance, where my laughter began.

The light waved at me, with a flick of its hand,
Inviting the flowers to join in the band.
With sparkles of joy, they twirled all around,
I followed their lead, without making a sound.

With the forest all glowing, I promised to stay,
In this whimsical world, where we laugh and play.
A symphony of giggles, forever it prances,
In the wild embrace of where the light dances.

Where Spirits Wander

In the woods where shadows play,
A squirrel steals my sandwich today.
With acorns tossed like tiny grenades,
I chase him through the leafy glades.

Frogs croak jokes with toads in the muck,
While I trip over roots, oh what luck!
The trees giggle on a gentle breeze,
As I stumble and laugh, mind at ease.

Enchantment in the Forest Depths

The pixies threw a tea party grand,
With mushrooms served on a leafy stand.
The fairies danced in mismatched shoes,
While I gawked at my muddy blues.

An owl winks, with wisdom to share,
As I twirl and topple without a care.
A caterpillar criticizes my dance,
But I just giggle at my own mischance.

Reverie beneath the Canopy

Beneath the boughs where sunlight peeks,
I hear the trees gossip for weeks.
Their branches wave like playful hands,
As I plot my escape from this land.

The shadows tease with whispers low,
While acorns plop down, put on a show.
I wonder if they see my dismay,
But the woods just chuckle, come what may.

Wandering through Verdant Hues

Through greenery thick, I twirl and spin,
While a rabbit bursts forth with a silly grin.
He challenges me to a hopping race,
And I find myself lost in the chase.

The breeze fans my hair in a chaotic dance,
As trees sway and whirl, oh what a chance!
I laugh with the flowers, who wink and sigh,
Telling me, "Stay a while, don't be shy!"

www.ingramcontent.com/pod-product-compliance
Lightning Source LLC
Chambersburg PA
CBHW070750220426
43209CB00083B/299